Women World Leaders

Stephen Currie

ReferencePoint Press®

San Diego, CA

For more information, contact:
ReferencePoint Press, Inc.
PO Box 27779
San Diego, CA 92198
www.ReferencePointPress.com

LIBRARY OF CONGRESS CATALOGING-IN-PUBLICATION DATA

Name: Currie, Stephen, 1960- author.
Title: Women world leaders / by Stephen Currie.
Description: San Diego, CA : ReferencePoint Press, Inc., [2016] | Series:
  Collective biographies | Includes bibliographical references and index.
Identifiers: LCCN 2015046498 (print) | LCCN 2015046983 (ebook) | ISBN
  9781682820346 (hardback) | ISBN 9781682820353 (epub)
Subjects: LCSH: Women--Political activity--Biography. | Women
  politicians--Biography. | Women heads of state--Biography.
Classification: LCC HQ1236 .C87 2016 (print) | LCC HQ1236 (ebook) | DDC
  320.082--dc23
LC record available at http://lccn.loc.gov/2015046498

CONTENTS

INTRODUCTION

Queens and Beyond

Through most of recorded history, the great bulk of government and political leaders have been male. That is no accident. In many societies before modern times—and some even today—leaders were chosen according to physical strength and the ability to fight. Because the average woman is not as strong as the average man, and because girls rarely received training in how to fight effectively, it was rare for a woman to become a leader in these societies. Other cultures have used elections to determine leaders, but until recently elections were equally unlikely to result in a woman being chosen. Women were seldom encouraged to participate in the political sphere, and societies frequently did not allow women to vote.

In some cultures, in contrast, leadership was hereditary: a child of a king or queen automatically inherited the throne. This practice was common during the European Middle Ages, for example. But in virtually every country, sons had priority over daughters. Only if there were no surviving sons might a daughter become the ruler. Even then, another male relative might commandeer the throne. In 1135, for example, Henry I of England died without sons. His daughter Matilda should have been queen, but her cousin Stephen seized power instead. Few women who lived under this hereditary system ever actually ruled a country.

Despite these obstacles, several women did become leaders in antiquity. The pharaohs who ruled ancient Egypt, for example, included women. The most famous of these, Cleopatra, was born into a royal family in 69 BCE. As a young woman, she led the country along with her father and a younger brother. Soon after their father died, Cleopatra decided to rule on her own. She enlisted the help of the Roman leader Julius Caesar, ousted her brother, and led Egypt for over twenty years.

Powerful Women

Like Cleopatra, a few later women leaders also wielded enormous influence and power. Queen Elizabeth I of England, for example, ruled from 1558 to 1603. "I will be as good unto ye as ever a Queen was unto her people,"[1] she promised her subjects upon taking the throne. Under Elizabeth's reign, England maintained its independence, displaced Spain as the world's primary seafaring power, and experienced a blossoming of the arts. The years of her monarchy are still referred to as the Elizabethan Era.

> "I will be as good unto ye as ever a Queen was unto her people."[1]
>
> —Queen Elizabeth I of England.

In the English-speaking world, Elizabeth is probably the best-known woman leader before modern times. There were others, however. Another powerful queen, Catherine the Great of Russia, ruled from 1762 to 1796. Catherine married Peter III, a Russian prince who later became the country's czar, or emperor. When her husband was assassinated, Catherine seized power with the support of army officers. As Elizabeth did with England, Catherine built up Russia's military and economy while supporting the arts. And Queen Isabella of Spain, who ruled jointly with her husband, King Ferdinand, was a strong leader remembered today mainly for giving Christopher Columbus the money he needed to sail west across the Atlantic Ocean.

One of the most well known women leaders in history is Cleopatra, who ruled Egypt in antiquity. This eighteenth century painting depicts Cleopatra displaying a bust of her ally, Roman leader Julius Caesar.

Europe was not alone in having female leaders before the 1900s. Between 1828 and 1861, for example, Ranavalona I was the queen of Madagascar off Africa's southeastern coast. Like Catherine, Ranavalona took power after the death of her husband, who had been king for eighteen years. She is best known today for keeping European powers from taking over Madagascar. Further back in history, the kingdom of Silla on the Korean Peninsula had three female rulers at various times. These included a woman named Seondeok, who ruled from 632 to 647 and sparked a rebirth of the arts in the region.

Moving Forward

By the mid-1900s the reluctance to allow women to lead was beginning to change. As the world moved away from monarchy and toward democratic elections, and as traditional gender roles began to change, it was increasingly common to find women vying for positions of power. In 1960 Sirimavo Bandaranaike was elected prime minister of Ceylon (now Sri Lanka), taking over for her murdered husband and becoming the first woman to be elected a world leader in modern times. "I would personally have preferred to keep away from politics and lead a quiet and secluded life," she said at the time. "But it is a duty which I owe to my late husband."[2] Later women leaders included Benazir Bhutto of Pakistan, Helen Clark of New Zealand, and Corazon Aquino of the Philippines.

Today the future for women leaders is bright. Countries as widely scattered as Brazil, Croatia, and South Korea have women as presidents or prime ministers. While as of 2015 no woman has been elected US president, several women have entered presidential races, and the fact that they are women seems unremarkable for most voters. In the years since Sirimavo Bandaranaike was elected in Ceylon, women have made enormous strides in politics and government. There is no reason to believe that this trend will end anytime soon.

> "I would personally have preferred to keep away from politics and lead a quiet and secluded life. But it is a duty which I owe to my late husband."[2]
>
> —Ceylonese prime minister Sirimavo Bandaranaike.

CHAPTER 1

Indira Gandhi

In 2012 a poll of experts identified India as one of the worst countries in the world for women and girls. Legally and culturally, Indian women enjoy fewer opportunities—and live in greater danger—than women in most of the developed world. Even today, for example, many girls are not given the opportunity to attend school, and women do not have the same rights to land and property as men. The incidence of rape is high, and about 70 percent of women are victimized by domestic violence. "In India," notes British expert Gulshun Rehman, "women and girls continue to be sold as chattels, married off as young as 10, burned alive as a result of dowry disputes and . . . exploited and abused as domestic slave labor."[3]

But in at least one way, Indian culture has been quite favorable to women. In most of the world, women leaders are a very recent phenomenon. Few countries had a woman leader before 1990; one exception was India. In 1966, members of India's Congress Party, a group made up overwhelmingly of men, voted to install a woman named Indira Gandhi as the party's leader. That action made Gandhi the country's prime minister—the person with the most power in the entire nation. She was then reelected with the support of the majority of the voters. Though women may not enjoy equal rights in modern India, the Indian people have chosen more than once to put a woman in charge of their government.

Early Life

When Indira Nehru was born on November 19, 1917, India was a British colony, unable to direct its own affairs or set policy that would benefit the people of the region. Many Indians were unhappy with British rule and agitated for Indian independence. Among these people were Indira's parents, especially her father, Jawaharlal Nehru. Trained as a lawyer, Nehru was deeply active in politics at the time of his daughter's birth. He led protests against the British government when she was young and became an outspoken force for change.

Young Indira's life, unfortunately, was less than idyllic. "I felt rather deprived of everything,"[4] she once told a journalist. Money was not the issue—though most of India's population lived in desperate poverty at the time, the Nehrus were well off. Instead, the problem was companionship. Indira's father was usually away from his home and family. Not only did he travel to gather support for the Indian cause, but he also spent nine years in jail during his daughter's childhood. Indira's mother, Kamala, was imprisoned once herself for political agitation and was in poor health while Indira was growing up. Indira's grandfather, whom she loved, died in 1931. Indira was an only child, and her family hired a private tutor to educate her; as a result, she rarely attended school.

> **"I felt rather deprived of everything."[4]**
>
> —*Indira Gandhi on her childhood.*

In 1934 Indira Nehru began university studies in India. Her mother, though, had become ill with tuberculosis. Medical care was generally better in Europe than in Asia, so Kamala Nehru arranged to travel to a sanitarium in Switzerland. Her health, however, did not permit her to travel alone. With Jawaharlal Nehru in prison, Indira was the only realistic choice, and she left school to accompany her mother. Kamala Nehru died in early 1936, just under a year after arriving in Europe. Rather than return to India right away, Indira Nehru enrolled at Oxford University.

Back to India

The people who knew Indira Nehru best during this time found her quiet and shy. At the same time, some noticed an inner strength that might have come from her difficult childhood. "She is like a little flower, which bends in the wind," a European woman wrote to Indira's father, attempting to describe his daughter, "but I think she will not break."[5] Indira was a solid student and an avid reader with a particular interest in the social sciences. When World War II broke out in 1939, though, she began to fear for her safety. She also began to believe that she should be back in India working toward independence for her people. In 1941, before earning a degree, she left Oxford and returned home.

Indira threw herself into the Indian independence movement upon her return. She also made time for romance. Feroze Gandhi, five years older than she, had been a longtime advocate of Indian independence. He had interrupted his own college career to work for India's self-determination. His political involvement had also brought him into close contact with Indira's parents—and with Indira herself. In 1942 Indira and Feroze married. Indira's father disapproved, citing differences in the couple's religious beliefs and arguing that Feroze's family was not wealthy enough, but he could not prevent the marriage. In the next few years the Gandhis had two sons—Rajiv, born in 1944, and Sanjay, two years younger.

As World War II raged, the United Kingdom had to devote most of its resources to the war effort. That left little energy to monitor what was happening in India. Anti-British forces in India took advantage of this inattention to push even harder for full independence. In 1947 they succeeded: India became a country in its own right, and Jawaharlal Nehru became the nation's first prime minister. He looked to his daughter to assist him. At first she mostly managed his personal business, dealing with correspondence and the like. But by 1952 she had moved into a

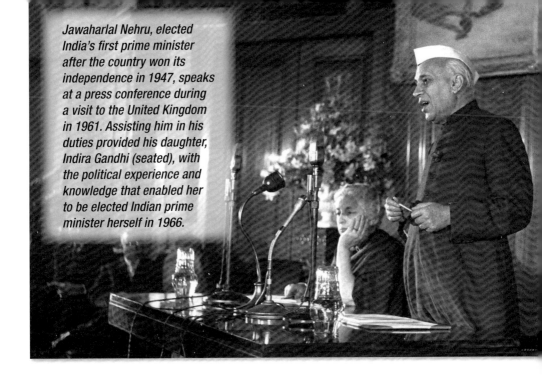

Jawaharlal Nehru, elected India's first prime minister after the country won its independence in 1947, speaks at a press conference during a visit to the United Kingdom in 1961. Assisting him in his duties provided his daughter, Indira Gandhi (seated), with the political experience and knowledge that enabled her to be elected Indian prime minister herself in 1966.

higher-profile position. She traveled with her father, arranged speaking engagements for him, and advised him on policy issues. Though she did not generally enjoy the socializing and small talk that went with this position, she rarely complained. "She knew that politics was something she could not escape,"[6] a friend said about her once.

Ready to Lead

Over time Indira Gandhi—the name by which she was now known—became more and more knowledgeable about Indian politics and government. She became increasingly sure of her abilities as well. In 1959 she ran for a leadership position in her father's Congress Party—and won. The job seemed to suit her; observers noted that she grew more confident and assertive in support of the policies she liked. The death of her husband in 1960 appeared to make her even more focused on her government work. As one biographer writes, it "caused her to move with increased momentum into the political scene."[7]

When Nehru died in 1964, some government officials suggested that his daughter should succeed him as prime minister

Sanjay and Rajiv Gandhi

Indira Gandhi's younger son, Sanjay, was originally considered the heir to the political dynasty begun by Indira Gandhi's father. Although Sanjay held no official position in Gandhi's government, in 1975 he became his mother's closest adviser. Some observers at the time believed that his influence over his mother was so strong that Sanjay in effect ran the government. Several members of Indira's cabinet resigned their posts to protest Sanjay's role in his mother's administration. Sanjay responded by helping his mother appoint new ministers who he felt would be more accepting of his influence.

In 1980 Sanjay was killed in a plane crash. His elder brother, Rajiv, had never had any interest in politics, but with Sanjay dead Indira pushed her elder son to play a greater role in government. In 1981 he was elected to a seat in parliament. When Indira Gandhi was assassinated three years later, Rajiv was appointed the next prime minister. However, Rajiv was killed by a suicide bomber in 1991—marking yet another violent death in the Gandhi family.

Today the family influence on Indian politics continues. Rajiv's widow, Sonia, has been a leader in India's Congress Party, and their son, Rahul, holds a parliamentary seat as well. As for Sanjay's family, his widow was appointed to the cabinet in 2014, and their son, Varun, is also in parliament. The two branches of the family no longer work in concert, though; Sanjay's widow and son represent a different party from Rajiv's.

and head of the Congress Party. That did not happen, and indeed many observers were appalled by the suggestion. Some believed that appointing the previous leader's daughter to the position would be undemocratic. Others scoffed at the notion that a woman could lead the Indian government. Still, Gandhi was intrigued by the notion that she might someday become prime minister. She accepted a cabinet post in the government led by her father's replacement, Lal Bahadur Shastri.

When Shastri died in 1966, Gandhi believed she was ready to lead the party as well as the nation. She took on the favored candidate, fellow Congress Party leader Morarji Desai. The winner would become the next prime minister; any party with more than half the legislative seats was entitled to choose the prime minister, and the Congress Party held a clear majority at the time of Shastri's death. The vote, which took place later in 1966, was close, but Gandhi won an unexpected victory. It helped her candidacy that she was the daughter of the popular Nehru, but she also impressed many party members with her intelligence and political skills. Her position became even more secure the following year when the Congress Party won another election: The voters of the country had agreed that Gandhi should be their prime minister.

Prime Minister

As prime minister, Gandhi generally took positions on the left of the political spectrum, championing socialist ideas such as nationalizing banks—that is, taking them out of private hands and having them run instead by the government. She was also interested in centralizing power. Like the United States, India has a federal system in which the national government shares authority with the states that make up the country. Before Gandhi's time, the states typically held more power than the federal government. Under Gandhi's administration, power began to move toward the national government. Since Gandhi led the federal government, that shift added to her own authority as well.

India's opposition parties worried that Gandhi was becoming too powerful. In addition, they objected to her socialist leanings. Gandhi's overall antipathy toward capitalism made them nervous, and they suspected that she might soon nationalize industries beyond banking. Even some members of Gandhi's own Congress Party feared that she was going too far. For a few of these colleagues, the possible outcomes of a continued Gandhi prime ministership seemed bleak indeed. "One of her fellow Congress Party members," a reporter noted soon after Gandhi's ascension to power, "has likened [her] to Kali, the Hindu goddess of destruction."[8] In 1969 several leaders of the Congress Party decided to throw Gandhi out of the party altogether.

The move backfired. Gandhi simply formed a new political organization together with her supporters from the existing Congress Party. Confusingly enough, this new group also was called the Congress Party. That gave India two Congress Parties, with Gandhi's being the larger of the two, and she maintained her grip on the prime minister's office. She easily won the 1971 election too, running with the slogan *Garibi Hatao*, or Eradicate Poverty; the opposition's slogan, which indicates the degree to which the country was split in its opinion of Gandhi, was *Indira Hatao*, or Remove Indira.

Gandhi could not eradicate poverty, of course. There were too many poor people to help them all. And the problems that caused poverty, such as lack of schooling and health care, could not be solved in just a few years. Nonetheless, Gandhi introduced several important measures designed to help India's poorest citizens. Not only did she help give them food, shelter, and clothing, but she made sure they had a voice, even if only a small one, in India's government. In the early 1970s Gandhi was one of the most popular people in India, admired by what appeared to be a majority of the country's citizens, though there was no shortage of Indians who objected to almost everything she did.

Trouble

That popularity did not last. Gandhi's political enemies charged her with corruption and electoral fraud, and in 1975 the country's Supreme Court agreed. The judges told her to forfeit her seat in the legislature and the prime minister's office as well. Backed by her supporters, Gandhi ignored the order. "The prime minister of India will continue in office until the electorate of India decides otherwise,"[9] said one of her advocates. Gandhi did indeed remain in office, in part by arresting dozens of her most vocal political opponents. She also declared a state of emergency, which allowed her to suspend elections and make laws without consulting the legislature. The remaining opposition was furious—India, said one leader, was entering "an era of darkness"[10]—but no one had the daring or the ability to remove her.

> "The prime minister of India will continue in office until the electorate of India decides otherwise."[9]
>
> —*Congress Party official B.K. Nehru.*

Gandhi lifted the state of emergency in 1977 and allowed elections again. She believed that the people would support her enthusiastically. But she was wrong. Once more, her party split in two—again, each group claimed the name of the Congress Party—over concerns about her policies and character. Opposition from all sides was intense: "End Dictatorship, Dethrone the Queen"[11] read one anti-Gandhi slogan.

This time, the election was a disaster for Gandhi. Her party was soundly defeated, she lost her seat in the legislature, and the leaders of the new government arrested her on charges that

This photo of Indira Gandhi was taken shortly before her death in 1984. Earlier, a standoff between government forces and members of the Sikh ethnic group resulted in many deaths among the latter. In retaliation, two of Gandhi's bodyguards, themselves Sikhs, assassinated her.

War with Pakistan

When the British colony of India became independent in 1947, its territory was divided into three parts. The largest, populated mainly by adherents of the Hindu religion, became the modern nation of India. The second- largest territory became West Pakistan, a majority Muslim country to India's west. The third territory, smaller than the others, was in the far eastern part of the colony. It was known as East Pakistan. Like West Pakistan, it had a largely Muslim population. Though they lacked a common border, the two Pakistans were joined together as one country.

The connection was an uneasy one. Despite the religious similarity, many people in East Pakistan did not feel much kinship with those in West Pakistan. Moreover, they believed that the West Pakistanis dominated the government and the economy. An independence movement began to grow. In 1970 the Pakistani government cracked down hard on the East Pakistani dissidents, leading to guerrilla warfare against the West Pakistani troops within East Pakistan. The following year East Pakistan declared itself independent and renamed the country Bangladesh. The declaration prompted attacks by the West Pakistanis.

Under Gandhi, India supported the Bangladeshis' independence movement but did not become involved in the fighting until Pakistan made the mistake of dropping bombs on Indian territory in December 1971. India quickly declared war on behalf of Bangladesh. Indian firepower made an enormous difference; in less than two weeks the war was over. Gandhi received a great deal of credit for the victory among India's population, and her Congress Party did extremely well in the next elections.

she had intended to kill some of her political opponents. She was put on trial but eventually acquitted. In 1980, having regained the support of many ordinary Indians who believed she had been treated unfairly, she ran again. This time she led her branch of the Congress Party to victory and became prime minister once more.

Trouble was brewing, however. In the early 1980s some leaders of an ethnic group called the Sikhs asked for greater autonomy in deciding their own affairs. Gandhi's government refused. The dispute culminated in a standoff between government forces and some of the most radical Sikhs, who had barricaded themselves in a temple. In the end, many of the Sikhs were killed. Most Sikhs were furious because of the massacre; some vowed revenge. In October 1984 Gandhi gave a speech in which she told her listeners, "I am alive today, I may not be there tomorrow. . . . I shall continue to serve until my last breath and when I die, I can say that every drop of my blood will invigorate India and strengthen it."[12] The next day, two Sikhs who served as Gandhi's bodyguards shot her to death.

Today, Indira Gandhi is well remembered both in India and in other nations. Her legacy is mixed. She was a strong advocate on behalf of the poor, and her policies strengthened India in important ways. At the same time, her decision to arrest opponents and declare a state of emergency was heavily criticized in India. Even today, Indian citizens are split on the subject of her overall effectiveness and her impact on the growth and stability of their country. Regardless, Gandhi earns credit for being one of the first woman leaders to appear on the world stage—and for having overcome enormous obstacles to do it.

> "I shall continue to serve until my last breath and when I die, I can say that every drop of my blood will invigorate India and strengthen it."[12]
>
> —*Indira Gandhi*

CHAPTER 2

Golda Meir

The modern country of Israel was established in 1948 as a homeland for the Jewish people of the world. Many people have been responsible for making Israel a nation—and for keeping it one in the face of hostility from some of its nearest neighbors. David Ben-Gurion, for example, guided Israel through its early years as the country's first prime minister. Yitzhak Rabin served as prime minister during some of Israel's most turbulent years and strengthened the country's ties with the United States. Moshe Dayan, a soldier and diplomat, was instrumental in making Israel a military power and was also involved in peace talks with other countries.

But no one played a greater role than Golda Meir. Founder, fund-raiser, and prime minister, Meir worked tirelessly on behalf of her country and is remembered today as the "strong-willed, straight-talking, gray-bunned grandmother of the Jewish people."[13] Without her, it is possible that Israel would not exist.

From Kiev to Milwaukee

Golda Meir was born Golda Mabovitch in Kiev in what is now Ukraine on May 3, 1898. Kiev was then in Russian territory, and the Jews of the region were persecuted by the Russian government and the Russian people. From time to time Russian leaders would order pogroms, or violent attacks, against Jewish settlements; these frequently ended in the massacre of most or all of the Jews in the vicinity. The Mabovitch family was no stranger to anti-Jewish sentiment or to anti-Jewish violence. One of Golda's first memories was of her father boarding up the family's doors to keep marauding Russian troops out of their house. Poverty was an issue as well: "I was always a little too cold outside and a little too empty inside,"[14] she said once.

> "I was always a little too cold outside and a little too empty inside."[14]
>
> —Golda Meir

In 1903 Moshe Mabovitch, Golda's father, left Europe for America. His intention was to work at whatever jobs he could find and then send for his wife and three daughters. He started off in New York City but soon found better opportunities farther west in Milwaukee, Wisconsin. By 1906 Moshe had saved enough to bring his family to Milwaukee. To supplement the family's income, Golda's mother opened a grocery store. Whenever she could not be at the store, she left it in the hands of Golda, who, though only eight years old, was competent and trustworthy.

Golda Mabovitch learned to speak fluent English, excelled in elementary school, and wanted to continue on to high school. Her parents preferred that she drop out and get married. Golda strenuously objected. Afraid her parents would force her to accede to their wishes, she ran away and traveled to Colorado to live instead with her older sister, Shayna. Shayna and her husband were deeply interested in ideas. They regularly invited friends to their house to discuss politics and other topics. Golda took part in these discussions and listened carefully when others spoke. "To the extent that my own future convictions were shaped and given form . . . while I was growing," she wrote years later, "those talk-filled nights in Denver played a considerable role."[15]

In 1913, having patched up the quarrel with her parents, Meir returned to Milwaukee. Over the next few years she finished high school, took college classes, and taught at a Yiddish-language school. In 1917 she married Morris Meyerson, a sign painter she had known for several years. The couple's future was not going to be in Milwaukee, however. For that matter, it would not be in the United States. Golda Meyerson—who would later change her name to Meir, the Hebrew version of her married name—had become part of a Jewish nationalist movement known as Zionism, and that involvement would dramatically change the course of her life.

A lifelong Zionist, or supporter of the establishment of a Jewish homeland, Golda Meir (pictured) played vital roles in the creation of the nation of Israel: fund-raiser, international advocate, and signer of the country's declaration of independence. Later, she served as foreign minister for ten years and as prime minister for five.

Zionism

Zionism first became popular among European Jews late in the 1800s. The aim of the movement was to establish a Jewish state, preferably in Palestine—the name given at the time to much of the Middle East just east of the Mediterranean Sea. This region had been the homeland of the ancient Israelites, and the Bible asserted that God had given it to the Jews. By the nineteenth century, though, comparatively few Jews lived in the Middle East. Over time other peoples, notably Arab Muslims, had pushed most Jewish families out of the area. A large number of Jews had eventually settled in central or eastern Europe. Many of these European Jews were treated poorly, as Meir knew from experience, and longed for a safe homeland.

Since Palestine was already occupied by other groups, it was impractical for hundreds of thousands of Jews to migrate there. Instead, Zionists encouraged individual Jews to move to Palestine. This strategy began to change in the late 1910s, though, when Britain took over Palestine from the former rulers, the Turkish-based Ottoman Empire. The British, unlike the Ottomans, had indicated that they might support a Jewish state.

It was with high hopes, then, that Meir and her husband left for Palestine in 1921. At first they lived on a communal farm called a kibbutz. Later they moved to the city of Jerusalem, where Meir's husband worked as a bookkeeper and Meir stayed home with the couple's two children. But though she was a loving mother—her son wrote years later that she was "attentive, kind, considerate, witty and a healer of wounds"[16]—Meir yearned to become more involved in the struggle for a Jewish state.

The Rise of the Nazis

Accordingly, in 1928 Meir took a job with a Jewish women's organization. From there she moved on to a position with Histadrut, an organization of Jewish trade unions. Other Histadrut members noticed her drive and intelligence, along with her knowledge of English, which most Jews from Europe did not speak. Histadrut began sending Meir on trips to the United States, where she spoke about the Jews' struggle in Palestine and encouraged American Jews to send money to help out. She soon became the head of Histadrut's political department, where her fluent English made her an effective liaison between the Palestinian Jews and the British government.

There was plenty of work for Meir to do, especially beginning in 1933, when Adolf Hitler's Nazi Party came to power in Germany. Germany had once been among the world's most tolerant countries regarding Judaism, but the virulently anti-Semitic Nazis drove out many of the country's Jews and eventually murdered most of the rest. The immediate result was an increase in the number of Jewish immigrants to Palestine. There had already been tension between Palestine's Jews and the region's Arabs, and now those tensions erupted into violence.

> "There is only one thing I hope to see before I die, and that is that my people should not need expressions of sympathy any more."[17]
>
> —Golda Meir

In the meantime, Hitler was moving toward war with Germany's neighbors. The possibility of living under Nazi rule alarmed Jews across Europe, and millions were desperate to leave. The question was where they could go. At a conference in 1938, held to discuss the issue, only one country, the Dominican Republic, agreed to expand the number of Europe's Jews it would accept. The refusals appalled Meir, who was an observer at the conference, and she was not mollified when delegates from other nations told her how sorry they were. "There is only one thing I hope to see before I die," she said, "and that is that my people should not need expressions of sympathy any more."[17]

The Birth of Israel

Palestine might have been a possible destination for the Jews fleeing from Nazism, but the British did not want to inflame the tensions between Arabs and Jews. Accordingly, they limited immigration to about fifteen thousand Jews a year—a tiny fraction of those who wished to leave. Meir unsuccessfully urged Britain

Meir and Moscow

Golda Meir served as an ambassador to the Soviet Union soon after Israel became independent. Soviet Jews had frequently been persecuted for their beliefs, and most Jews rarely attended religious services. When she attended a service for the high holiday of Rosh Hashanah, Meir was shocked to discover the impact she had on the Jews of Moscow. As she wrote in her memoir:

> The street in front of the synagogue had changed. Now it was filled with people, packed together like sardines, hundreds and hundreds of them, of all ages, including Red [Soviet] Army officers, soldiers, teenagers and babies carried in their parents' arms. Instead of the 2,000-odd Jews who usually came to the synagogue on the holidays, a crowd of close to 50,000 people was waiting. . . . They had come—these good, brave Jews—in order to be with us, to demonstrate their sense of kinship and to celebrate the establishment of the State of Israel. Within seconds, they had surrounded me, almost lifting me bodily, almost crushing me, saying my name over and over again. Eventually, they parted ranks and let me enter the synagogue, but there, too, the demonstration went on. Every now and then, in the women's gallery, someone would come to me, touch my hand, stroke or even kiss my dress. . . . The Jews of Moscow were proving their profound desire—and their need—to participate in the miracle of the establishment of the Jewish state, and I was the symbol of the state for them.

Golda Meir, *My Life*. New York: Putnam, 1975, p. 250.

to increase that number. Indeed, the British now seemed to be working against the Zionists. In 1940 British leaders in Palestine passed a law forbidding Jews from buying property in the vast majority of the territory. Meir was horrified—and furious.

World War II ended in 1945 with the near extermination of Europe's remaining Jews. About 6 million died in Hitler's concentration camps during what is now called the Holocaust. Many of the survivors tried to reach Palestine, but were kept out by Britain. Anti-British riots broke out among Palestine's Jews. Before long, Britain had had enough. Its government appealed to the United Nations, a newly formed organization of the world's countries, to decide what should happen to Palestine. Because of the horror of the Holocaust and concern that Jews were not truly safe in any existing country, the UN voted to establish a new Jewish state: Israel.

The decision delighted Meir and her fellow Zionists. But the news was sobering as well. The surrounding countries, they knew, would be enraged at the idea of a Jewish state in the region. It would be necessary to have weapons to defend against a possible attack. Once again, Meir was chosen to solicit money from Jewish Americans. Some Zionist leaders believed that she would collect no more than $10 million, but Meir raised $50 million for the nation's military. In May 1948 she became one of just twenty-four people to sign Israel's declaration of independence. "After I signed, I cried,"[18] she remembered afterward. It had been a long struggle, but Israel was now an independent country.

War and Peace

In 1949 Meir was elected to a seat in the Knesset, or legislature. She joined the prime minister's cabinet as well, initially serving as Minister of Labor and National Insurance. In this position she was instrumental in building roads, houses, and schools, and in helping to integrate hundreds of thousands of newcomers into Israeli society. In 1956 she was appointed foreign minister, one of the highest-ranking positions in the Israeli government. As foreign minister she worked with diplomats and leaders of other nations to form alliances with various countries, including the United States; she also helped plan strategy during a war with Egypt. Few other Israelis were as well known—or as well liked—as Meir at this point.

Meir resigned from the cabinet in 1966, hoping to enjoy a slower pace of life as she entered her later years. But that was not to be, as her party's leader, prime minister Levi Eshkol, died suddenly in 1969. Needing a new leader—and a new prime minister—the party turned to Meir. Her tenure as prime minister lasted just five years, but those years were of great importance for Israel's survival. Recognizing that the frequent attacks by

Meir worked tirelessly for peace in hopes of achieving security for Israel. Pictured here with American diplomat Henry Kissinger and his mother, Paula, Meir remains today one of the best-loved Israeli leaders.

neighboring Arab countries were deeply damaging to Israel, Meir worked especially hard for peace. She met with a variety of world leaders, including the pope, to get support for peace talks. She was willing to compromise too, agreeing to shrink Israel's boundaries slightly in order to placate Arabs who also claimed the land.

But peace was a difficult goal. In October 1973 Meir received information that troops from Egypt and Syria were gathering near their respective borders with Israel. The reports worried Meir. She feared that both countries might be planning an attack, and her instinct was to mobilize Israel's army. Meir's advisers, however, doubted that war was imminent. The last major war against the Arabs had taken place in 1967, after Egypt had attacked Israel, and it had ended with an Israeli victory. The advisers did not believe their neighbors would risk another invasion. They carried the day, and Meir did not order the Israeli army to get ready for a possible war.

Within hours, though, new intelligence reports indicated that both Syria and Egypt were indeed about to invade Israel. Meir briefly considered launching an attack on the Syrians before their troops entered Israel, but rejected the idea. She suspected that the United States, Israel's closest ally, would disapprove of a strike against Syria and might withhold its support. "If we strike first," she said, "we won't get help from anybody."[19] Instead, she quickly mobilized the Israeli military—but too late for them to repel the attack. Due largely to this lack of preparedness, the war began badly for the Israelis.

Stepping Down

The conflict, known as the Yom Kippur War because it started on the Jewish holiday of Yom Kippur, lasted close to a month. In the end, Israel beat back the invaders. Though several thousand Israelis were killed and the country lost a small piece of land to Egypt, most observers agreed that Israel had won the war. But Meir's handling of the conflict was widely criticized. Many Israelis blamed her for not calling up the military as soon as she knew that Arab troops were at the borders. "How could we have been so unready?"[20] one soldier demanded of Meir. A senior military officer likewise publicly singled out Meir for the loss of his troops, many of whom had been killed by the enemy in the surprise attack.

Not everyone held Meir responsible. A special government commission, asked to investigate, placed the largest share of the blame on Israel's military intelligence and concluded that Meir was not at fault. Indeed, commission members praised her for mobilizing Israeli troops when she did. Meir received another vote of confidence when her party won the next national election, allowing her to continue as prime minister. Quite a few Israelis recognized that Meir was not a military expert; the error, in their view, lay more with Meir's advisers than with the prime minister herself.

Still, criticism continued. In 1974, tired of defending herself and feeling as though she had done all she could as prime minister, Meir resigned. "Five years are sufficient," she said. "It is beyond my strength to continue carrying this burden."[21] In retirement, she wrote her autobiography and collected many awards in appreciation of her years of service to Israel. In particular, Meir was given the country's highest honor, the Israel Prize. It was a fitting award for a woman who had done so much to help her country. Meir died at the age of eighty in 1978 and still ranks among the most famous—and best loved—of Israeli leaders.

> "It is beyond my strength to continue carrying this burden."[21]
>
> —*Golda Meir*

CHAPTER 3

Margaret Thatcher

Before the twentieth century, few countries could equal Great Britain's record for female heads of state. Not once but twice, England had been ruled by strong—and very popular—queens: Elizabeth I from 1558 to 1603, and Victoria from 1837 to 1901. Nonetheless, Britain had very few women politicians through most of the 1900s. In 1930, for example, there were just three women in the 615-member House of Commons, which made up one of the two branches of Parliament—Britain's legislative body—and none at all in the smaller House of Lords. Even in the 1960s and early 1970s, when female legislators became more common, the idea that a woman might someday be elected head of government seemed completely implausible to many Britons. "I don't think there will be a woman prime minister in my lifetime,"[22] predicted member of Parliament Margaret Thatcher during an interview in 1973.

But Thatcher was wrong. Just two years after that interview, Thatcher became the leader of Britain's influential Conservative Party. In Britain's parliamentary system, whichever party wins the most seats in an election gets to choose the prime minister—who is almost always the person who is the leader of the party at the time of the vote. When the Conservatives won the national election in 1979, Thatcher became prime minister—the most powerful person in British government, and one of the most powerful in the world.

Science and Politics

Margaret Roberts was born in the British town of Grantham on October 13, 1925. She came from a working-class family: her mother was a dressmaker and her father owned a grocery store. Her father was also involved in politics, at one point running for mayor, and young Margaret was doing campaign work by the time she was ten. "Politics," she would later say, "was in my bloodstream."[23] Though her father had not gone to high school, Margaret was determined to graduate from college. An avid reader, she studied hard in school and particularly enjoyed science, government, and law. In 1943, her efforts paid off; she was admitted to Oxford University.

At university, Margaret focused on science, eventually graduating from Oxford with two degrees in chemistry. In 1947 she moved into the workforce and obtained employment as a research scientist. She soon came to realize, though, that government was more interesting to her than science. She was already active in Conservative Party politics. At Oxford she had led the university's Conservative Association. Recognizing Margaret's drive and intelligence, party leaders asked her to run for a House of Commons seat during the 1950 election. She was happy to oblige, and she stood out among other Conservatives running that year. "Once she opened her mouth," fellow Conservative candidate Bill Deedes recalled ruefully, "the rest of us began to look rather second-rate."[24]

> "I don't think there will be a woman prime minister in my lifetime."[22]
>
> —Margaret Thatcher

Even so, Margaret had little chance of winning her race. The district where she was running leaned heavily toward the Labour Party, the other main British political party at the time. Still, she lost by fewer votes than many people expected. She ran again in the same district during the election of 1951, but the numbers were still against her: for the second time, she lost to the Labour candidate.

After this second defeat, Margaret temporarily gave up her political ambitions. Early in 1949 she had met a businessman named Denis Thatcher at a political function. The two saw each other when their busy schedules permitted, and shortly after the 1951 election the couple married. Though Denis Thatcher remained largely in the background during his wife's political ca-

Margaret Thatcher is pictured with her twins, Mark and Carol, who were born in 1953. After the children entered school, Thatcher ran for a House of Commons seat despite two previous election losses. This time, in 1959, she won.

reer, he was always supportive of her ambitions. "I could never have been Prime Minister," Margaret Thatcher wrote, "without Denis by my side."[25]

Margaret Thatcher earned a legal degree in 1953. The same year the couple had twins, Mark and Carol; they would be the Thatchers' only children. By the late 1950s the children were in school and Thatcher was ready to resume her activities in government. Some party leaders tried to dissuade her from running for a legislative seat. One man told her that she needed to stay home with her children. Thatcher was not inclined to take their advice. "If you want something said, ask a man," she said once in response to those who did not take her seriously because she was female. "If you want something done, ask a woman."[26] In any case, other party leaders were more encouraging. In 1959 Thatcher ran in a pro-Conservative district—and won.

> "If you want something said, ask a man; if you want something done, ask a woman."[26]
>
> —Margaret Thatcher

Moving Up

In the British system it can be difficult for new legislators to make a name for themselves. Thatcher, however, impressed party leaders. Before long, she was appointed secretary for education and science, a post that won her attention beyond her district and party. Her work in this position was controversial. Charged with cutting education budgets in a time when finances were tight, Thatcher eliminated free milk for elementary students. This decision was extremely unpopular; people shouted her down at public forums, wrote negative letters to the newspapers about her, and called her the "Milk Snatcher."[27]

Thatcher was not discouraged by these responses. On the contrary, the opposition she faced seemed to strengthen her resolve. As a Conservative, Thatcher embraced private enterprise, low taxes, low government spending, and other measures that she believed encouraged hard work and independence. She strongly opposed trade unions, which made up the foundation of the Labour Party, and viewed welfare payments and immigration with suspicion.

As time passed, Thatcher became concerned that her party's leadership was not fighting hard enough for her conservative goals. As a result, she ran for Conservative Party leader in 1975. The Conservatives were not in power at the time, but by becoming party leader Thatcher would become prime minister if her party won the next election. All Conservative members of the House of Commons took part in the voting, and Thatcher won on the second ballot. The next national election took place in May 1979 during an economic slowdown punctuated by a series of strikes. The Conservative Party won well over half the available seats. Margaret Thatcher had achieved what she once thought impossible: becoming Britain's first woman prime minister.

Controversy

Thatcher's tenure as prime minister began with controversy. Though very popular among members of her own party, she was deeply disliked by Labour supporters. Their dislike became more pronounced when Thatcher began her term by sharply cutting government budgets. By this time, Britain had developed a strong social safety net in which generous government benefits were available to the unemployed, senior citizens, and other groups who struggled financially. Thatcher believed that these benefits were excessive, that they destroyed initiative on the part of ordinary Britons, and that maintaining them required well-off Britons to pay too much in taxes. During the campaign, she had not concealed her distaste for these payments.

Still, many Britons were appalled when Thatcher proposed reducing or even eliminating these benefits. The effects of cutting the social safety net would fall disproportionately on the poor. Thatcher had earlier been vilified for taking away milk; now anti-Thatcher rhetoric grew stronger and more hostile. The relationship between Thatcher and her opponents became even more strained when Thatcher began selling government-owned industries and services to corporations. Many forms of public transportation, for example, became the responsibility of private

Margaret Thatcher and Ronald Reagan

Though Thatcher often rejected previous British policies, her approach to both foreign and domestic issues was in some ways very much in keeping with the times. In 1980 voters in the United States overwhelmingly chose former California governor Ronald Reagan to be the nation's next president. Reagan, who served for two terms, was in most respects the most conservative American president in many years. He shared Thatcher's enthusiasm for cutting the size and reach of government, scaling back social benefits, privatizing industry, and attacking unions; he also shared Thatcher's perspective on communism and the Soviet Union.

The two leaders got along well both personally and professionally. "[Thatcher] certainly liked Reagan a lot from the moment he won office and he felt the same," says historian Julian Zelizer. "They had a deep respect, admiration and a friendship." They did not always agree on issues; Reagan was not convinced at first that the Falkland Islands war was a good idea, and Thatcher was frustrated by Reagan's willingness to allow the United States to pile up enormous debt. Nevertheless, they typically presented a united front toward other world leaders who did not share their perspectives on government. One person who knew their relationship well described them as "political soulmates."

Quoted in Halimah Abdullah, "Reagan and Thatcher: 'Political Soulmates,'" CNN, April 9, 2013. www.cnn.com.

companies under Thatcher's governance. Labour supporters charged that selling off services and industries would raise prices while enriching those who were already wealthy.

Thatcher also drew heavy criticism when she took steps to diminish the importance of trade unions. In her view, unions had entirely too much power and most union workers were overpaid. Thatcher saw unions as a particular problem in industries, such as coal mining, that were owned by the government. In her opinion, previous governments had been too quick to give in when industrial workers threatened to strike. Thatcher resolved, therefore, to take a harder line with organized labor. In 1984, for example, when most British coal miners went on strike in a dispute over lost jobs and mine closures, Thatcher refused to meet the miners' demands. The miners eventually returned to work under Thatcher's terms, and the power of their union had been severely damaged.

The Soviets and the Falklands

Thatcher was also noted for the zeal with which she opposed communism, a political and economic system most associated at the time with the Soviet Union (much of which is now Russia). Unlike the UK, the United States, and other democracies, the Soviet Union was a one-party state in which there were no free elections. The Soviet Union had a large arsenal of weapons, including nuclear warheads, and during Thatcher's time in office there was constant worry of a potential attack. Tensions between

"A Day I Was Not Meant to See"

One of the biggest issues facing Margaret Thatcher in her time as prime minister had to do with the Irish Republican Army (IRA), a terrorist group that carried out a number of attacks on British soil. The United Kingdom governed six counties in the northeastern part of Ireland, and IRA members, focused on reuniting the entire island under the Irish flag, were willing to use violence to persuade Britain to pull out of Ireland altogether. In 1979, for example, Thatcher's friend and political ally Airey Neave—a staunch opponent of the IRA and its demands—was killed in a car bomb explosion carried out by IRA members.

Thatcher was no more willing to bargain with the IRA than Neave had been, and in 1984 a group of IRA operatives decided to try to assassinate her. On October 12 of that year they set off a bomb at the Conservative Party's annual conference, held at a hotel in a seaside resort town. The resulting blast killed five people and injured many others, but Thatcher was unhurt. "This is a day I was not meant to see," she said in a speech the following afternoon. "The fact that we are gathered here, now, shocked but composed and determined, is a sign not only that this attack has failed, but that all attempts to destroy democracy by terrorism will fail." Still, it was a close call indeed, and the incident shook Britons deeply.

Quoted in John Bingham, "Margaret Thatcher: Seconds from Death at the Hands of an IRA Bomber," *Telegraph* (London), April 8, 2013. www.telegraph.co.uk.

the Soviet Union and the democratic countries of the West never did spill over into direct warfare but were high enough that the conflict was widely known as the Cold War.

Earlier British governments had tried to work with the Soviets, but Thatcher rejected this approach. "The Russians," she said in a famous speech, "are bent on world dominance, and they are rapidly acquiring the means to become the most powerful imperial nation the world has seen. . . . [This] is a time when we urgently need to strengthen our defences."[28] In her opinion, the Soviets needed to understand that the use of force on their part would be met with equal force from the UK and its allies. Thatcher won praise for this stance from people both in Britain and abroad. Others feared that her unwillingness to work with the Soviets might make an attack more likely.

Although the UK and the Soviet Union never went to war, Thatcher did wage war against another country during her term in office. The Falkland Islands, a lightly populated group of islands off the South American coast, had been a British possession for many years. Argentina, however, claimed the islands as well. In April 1982 Argentine forces invaded the Falklands. Britain fought back, quickly driving

> "We fought to show aggression does not pay."[29]
>
> —Margaret Thatcher

the Argentine forces off the islands, and the Falklands remained in the possession of the United Kingdom. The victory boosted Thatcher's popularity at home.

Thatcher's supporters and opponents had different views of her motives for fighting in the Falklands. Some believed that Thatcher only reluctantly went to war: She recognized that the financial and human cost of combat could be enormous, but could not allow an attack on British territory. "We fought to show aggression does not pay,"[29] she explained at one point. Others argued that Thatcher was motivated mainly by her low popularity at the time. In this view, she waged war to improve her chances of winning the next election. Historically, people are often reluctant to vote leaders out of office during or just after a war.

More Elections

Thanks to the British victory in the Falklands and to Thatcher's cuts to government programs, taxes, and spending, the Conservatives won the 1983 election, and Thatcher remained prime minister. Her second term, like her first, was marked by a continued focus on making cuts—cuts denounced by the increasingly frustrated opposition. In 1987 another election was held, and Thatcher retained her position. Before long, however, public opinion began to shift against Thatcher. Even some of her supporters worried that she had gone too far in turning government services over to private ownership. Others were beginning to tire of her conviction that she was always right. Still others were ready for a change in leadership; Thatcher, after all, was beginning her third term.

In the next two years confidence in Thatcher continued to drop. In 1990 a fellow conservative named David Heseltine challenged her for the party's leadership. Though she won a majority of the votes on the first ballot, Thatcher did not have enough support to win the election outright; she needed significantly more than half the votes to retain leadership. Recognizing that Thatcher had lost support among party members, her advisers encouraged her to resign rather than risk tearing the party in two. Feeling devastated and betrayed, Thatcher nonetheless felt obligated to follow their advice. Her tenure as prime minister was over.

Thatcher remained active in politics and government for some years after resigning her post as prime minister. She was delighted to watch the Soviet Union break apart in 1990–1991; the West, it was clear, had won the Cold War. Thatcher served out the rest of her term in Parliament. Later, she was a member of the House of Lords, the unelected wing of Parliament with much less power than the House of Commons. She worked for an American tobacco company, set up a foundation to support causes she valued—notably advocating for a strong national defense, free trade among nations, and greater contact between the nations of the West and those of the Middle East—and spoke frequently on political issues.

As time passed Thatcher began to suffer from health issues. In 2002, after several small strokes, she cut back on public speak-

Thatcher converses with Soviet leader Mikhail Gorbachev at a conference in Paris in 1990. By the time this photograph was taken, the Soviet Union was breaking up. An avowed anti-Communist, Thatcher was delighted with this evidence that the West had won the so-called Cold War with the Soviets.

ing. The following year, Denis Thatcher died. Despite developing dementia several years later, Margaret Thatcher still managed to make an occasional appearance until about 2009, when she moved out of the public eye for good. She died in 2013 at the age of eighty-seven.

Perhaps unsurprisingly, Thatcher's legacy has been as controversial as her life. Her political opponents continue to blame Thatcher for reducing benefits, attacking labor unions, and privatizing government services. Her supporters, in contrast, call her one of the best prime ministers in British history—for many of the same reasons. In either case, Thatcher is considered one of the most influential government leaders of her time. As much as any other leader of the late twentieth century, Margaret Thatcher helped change the world.

CHAPTER 4

Angela Merkel

For most of its history, Europe has been divided into many small countries. To bring the continent closer together, many of Europe's countries have formed an organization called the European Union (EU). While the member countries of the EU have kept their own governments, they cooperate in ways never seen before on the European continent. Though governance of the EU is shared by the member countries, one leader stands out as the most influential. That is Germany's chancellor, Angela Merkel. Merkel has worked tirelessly to make Europe financially strong, secure from its enemies, and an example of how different nations and governments can cooperate to everyone's benefit. For these reasons, Merkel has been called "Europe's quiet leader"[30] and the continent's "most powerful political figure."[31]

East and West

Angela Kasner came into the world on July 17, 1954. She was born in Hamburg, a city in northwestern Germany, but when she was just a few months old, her father, a minister, accepted a position in Templin, a town north of Berlin. Geographically speaking, the move was fairly insignificant. The Kasner family was only about a three-hour drive from Angela's birthplace in Hamburg, and German was spoken in both communities. On the surface the only important difference between the two communities seemed to be size: Hamburg was one of Europe's most populous and thriving cities, while Templin had fewer than twenty thousand inhabitants.

But the differences between Hamburg and Templin were in fact enormous. After World War II, Germany had been partitioned into two separate countries. The western and southern regions of the country, including Hamburg, became a new nation called West Germany. With a democratic form of government and an economy based largely on free markets, West Germany quickly became allied with countries such as the United States and the United Kingdom. The region that included Templin, in contrast, became the nation of East Germany. Closely connected to the Soviet Union, East Germany was a Communist country with a sluggish economy, shortages of consumer goods, and little personal freedom.

Under these circumstances, the Kasners' move from West Germany to East Germany was unusual. Angela's mother strongly opposed the move, but her father, who believed he could rise to a position of greater responsibility in the East than in the West, overruled his wife. The Kasners held a somewhat privileged position within East German society: they owned two cars, for example, when the vast majority of East German families had one at most. At the same time, the family's West German roots made some of their neighbors suspicious that they might be spies. Perhaps as a result, Angela's mother, a skilled English teacher, was never able to get a job.

Scientific Study

Angela Kasner paid little attention to the political situation in East Germany as she was growing up. "There was no shadow over my childhood,"[32] she said many years later. Focused on academics more than on making friends or becoming involved in extracurricular activities, Angela was recognized early on for her intellectual abilities. She did extremely well in high school, becoming a

German chancellor Angela Merkel (pictured) has been influential within the European Union leadership and beyond. Although Merkel studied and pursued a career in chemistry, she entered politics in 1990 after the fall of the Berlin Wall and the collapse of communism in East Germany.

fluent speaker of Russian and excelling in math and science. It was clear that she would go on to college.

Here, however, politics intruded. East German leaders had established a Communist organization called the Free German Youth. Many of the nation's young adults were active members in the group. Technically no one was required to join, but in practice it was difficult to gain admission to any East German university without being a member of the organization. As a result, Angela became a part of the organization. Years later, this decision would prove controversial. While many Germans believed that her decision to join the group was based more on pragmatism than on political philosophy, some charged that a person who had once supported a totalitarian government was not qualified to lead a democratic nation.

Angela excelled in college just as she had in high school. Her main focus was science; she earned a doctoral degree in chemistry and got a job at a state-run laboratory where she did research. "She really wanted to achieve something,"[33] says a former colleague, noting that most of her colleagues did not work nearly as hard as Angela. While employed at the lab, she published papers on various topics in chemistry. In 1977, early in her professional career, she also married a fellow scientist named Ulrich Merkel. The marriage did not last; the couple divorced in 1982. There were no children.

Though Merkel enjoyed science, her job was frustrating. During her adolescence, East Germany had quite literally walled itself off from much of the rest of the world. Concerned about the number of professionals who were emigrating, the East German government built walls on the country's borders with West Germany in 1961 and posted armed sentries to make sure no one could leave. East Germany also shielded its citizens from non-Communist ideas by banning Western publications, even scientific journals. Merkel suspected that science in the West was substantially ahead of science in the East, but she had no way of knowing exactly what Western scientists were doing. In any case, the science she was working on was clearly not cutting-edge.

> "She really wanted to achieve something."[33]
>
> —Former colleague of Angela Merkel.

The Walls Come Down

Merkel's life—and the lives of East Germans in general—changed dramatically in 1989, when the East German government unexpectedly relaxed its rules against immigration to the West. Antigovernment demonstrations followed. Late that fall, the walls separating East and West Germany came down, and the Communist government collapsed. When the barriers first opened,

Person of the Year

The year 2015 was eventful and difficult in Europe. Early in the year, sluggish economic growth and poor financial planning made it impossible for Greece to pay its debts. If Greece defaulted on its loans, most of them made by wealthier European countries, the entire EU would have suffered economically. Not long afterward, refugees from warfare in North Africa and the Middle East began pouring onto European shores. The majority of these newcomers were arriving with few if any possessions, and nearly all were in great need of assistance. The Greek economic crisis and the flood of refugees both threatened to overwhelm Europe.

Led by Angela Merkel, European leaders acted quickly in each case to prevent disaster. Merkel hammered out a deal with Greece in which many of the country's loans would be forgiven or restructured, averting a far-reaching financial crisis. She also worked tirelessly to encourage EU nations to offer new homes to refugees, with Germany alone accepting hundreds of thousands of newcomers, and other countries heeding Merkel's call to respond with kindness to the refugees.

In December 2015 *Time* magazine recognized Merkel's achievements by naming her its "Person of the Year"—the newsmaker with the greatest impact on world events. "It's pretty easily Angela Merkel," said *Time* editor Karl Vick. "Her response to [the refugees] was extraordinary. . . . You have the future of Europe at play, and her at the helm." Merkel was just the fourth woman to win the award as an individual since *Time* instituted it in 1927.

Quoted in Greg Botelho and Tim Hume, "*Time* Magazine Names German Leader Angela Merkel Its Person of the Year," CNN.com, December 9, 2015. www.cnn.com.

hundreds of thousands of East Germans joyfully poured into the West for an all-night celebration, but Merkel went to her health club—her usual routine for a Thursday night—and ventured only briefly over the border. "She had one beer and phoned an aunt in West Germany, then went home,"[34] writes a journalist.

East Germany clearly needed a new government, and few East Germans wanted another Communist regime. The question was how best to establish democratic principles in a land with no recent history of freedom. The country quickly split into multiple political parties. Though Merkel had little background in politics and none whatever in governing, she joined a party called the

Democratic Awakening, a relatively conservative party that had close connection to German churches, championed free-market ideals, and strongly supported the idea that the two Germanys should become one nation.

Merkel's party soon ran into trouble: The leader of the party, it was discovered, had served the Communist government as an undercover informant for the police. Casting around for someone calm, efficient, and articulate to deal with the breaking news, other party officials deputized Merkel to speak to the crowd of reporters gathering outside the office. Merkel did such a good job that she was immediately appointed chief spokesperson for the party. The Democratic Awakening did poorly in East Germany's first free elections, held in 1990, but Merkel had acquitted herself so well that she was given a similar public relations role in the new government. Impressed with her work, other East Germans encouraged her to continue in politics.

Despite the Democratic Awakening's loss, party leaders did have something else to applaud soon after the election: as the Democratic Awakening had advocated, East and West Germany officially merged later in 1990 to form a new German nation. Merkel, still interested in politics, joined the Christian Democratic Union (CDU), a West German party with leanings similar to those of the Democratic Awakening. She ran for a seat in the Bundestag, Germany's parliament, under the CDU banner—and won. Her political career was formally under way.

The CDU won a majority of seats in the 1990 election, and Helmut Kohl, the chancellor (the equivalent of a prime minister), made Merkel part of his cabinet. Her first assignment was as Minister for Women and Youth. Merkel's gender helped her earn this assignment, especially because the CDU did not have many women in the Bundestag. It also was helpful that she came from the former East Germany; Kohl recognized that for reasons of balance he would need to include East Germans in leadership positions. After four years in this role, she was moved to a different cabinet position, Minister for the Environment and Nuclear Safety. In 1998, toward the end of her tenure in this post, Merkel

Merkel speaks with German chancellor Helmut Kohl, who won election in 1990, at a Christian Democratic Union (CDU) Party meeting. Merkel served in Kohl's cabinet during his eight years in office but later called for him to resign from the CDU in the wake of a campaign finance scandal.

married again, this time to a professor of quantum chemistry named Joachim Sauer. A former East German like Merkel, Sauer had two sons from a previous marriage. Besides these two step-sons, Merkel has no children.

Merkel and Schröder

In 1998, the same year Merkel and Sauer married, new elections were held. This time Kohl and the CDU were defeated by their main opponents, the more liberal Social Democratic Party. Merkel left the cabinet, remaining in the Bundestag and serving in a position of leadership within the CDU. She was angry, however. The new chancellor, Gerhard Schröder, had publicly criticized Merkel's performance as the person in charge of nuclear issues, and she took the criticism personally. "I will put him in the corner, just like he did with me," she promised in an interview. "One day the time will come for this, and I am already looking forward."[35]

The time came sooner than most people expected. In 1999 the news broke that several CDU politicians had violated campaign finance laws. Among those implicated were Kohl and his successor as the chairman of the party, Wolfgang Schäuble. The scandal threatened to cut deeply into the CDU's votes in the next election. Many CDU members believed that Kohl and Schäuble needed to leave their posts for the good of the party, but the two showed no interest in stepping down. Because both men were powerful, moreover, most other members of the Bundestag were reluctant to speak up against them.

That was not true of Merkel, however. She wrote a bold newspaper opinion piece calling for the CDU to find replacements for the two men if they refused to resign. The article was influential, galvanizing public opinion both inside and outside of the party against Kohl and Schäuble. Recognizing the reality of the situation, Kohl and Schäuble agreed to leave their positions in early 2000. When the Christian Democrats gathered to elect new leaders, they chose Merkel to be the new party chair.

That made Merkel the CDU's candidate for chancellor in early 2005, when Schröder, still in power, called for new elections later that year. The campaign season was intense. Merkel and Schröder disliked each other professionally and personally, and the rhetoric of the campaign was bitter. Merkel argued for a greater emphasis on the free market; Schröder called for more government control of the economy. Schröder was insistent that Germany not join the United States in its war against Iraq; Merkel was willing to consider the possibility. Merkel wanted to cut back on social welfare programs; Schröder disagreed. The voting was close, but in the end the CDU won. Merkel had gotten her revenge on Schröder and become Germany's first woman chancellor.

Successes

For the most part, Merkel has been remarkably successful in this position. Though her critics sometimes say that she lacks a strong vision for Germany—"she [rejects] ideology and is prone

45

to switching course,"[36] a journalist wrote—her policies and decisions are usually in tune with public opinion. She has been moderately conservative in her politics—liberal enough to mollify voters who are slightly left of center and conservative enough to earn the trust of voters to her right on the political spectrum. She appears to have a high level of support among voters and the CDU. As of 2015 there were no serious challengers to her leadership from members of her own party.

> "She [rejects] ideology and is prone to switching course."[36]
>
> —Journalist on Angela Merkel.

And Merkel has been successful in many of her actions. Some of these successes involve domestic policy. When she took office, Germany, along with the rest of the world, was doing well economically. In 2008, when a recession hit across the globe, Germany was much less affected by the downturn than most other countries, thanks in part to Merkel's leadership. In 2015, when brutal civil wars caused many people in the Middle East to leave their home countries, Merkel welcomed hundreds of thousands of these refugees to Germany. For her, offering help was a moral imperative. "There can be no tolerance of those who question the dignity of other people,"[37] she told opponents of this policy.

Merkel has been especially prominent where foreign policy is concerned. She is a strong supporter of Israel and an advocate of close ties between Germany and the United States. But her greatest strengths have come in her dealings with other European countries, especially members of the EU. She has argued that Europe must become more competitive economically and has urged European countries to give up some of their more expensive social programs. She has also taken the lead in dealing with financial crises within the EU. On several occasions, for example, EU member nations have had difficulty paying their debts. More than any other leader, Merkel has dealt with the situation and hammered out a broadly acceptable solution.

What the future holds for Merkel is anyone's guess. As of 2016 she shows no sign of giving up her post, nor do the voters

Family

Merkel is known for her simple lifestyle and her desire for privacy. She and her husband continue to live in the same central Berlin apartment they owned when they married in 1998; her husband's name appears on the buzzer by the front door, but Merkel's does not. Other than Sauer's name, there is no indication that one of the most powerful leaders in the world lives at that address. Merkel and Sauer spend most of their free time at home and are rarely seen in public. When they attend concerts or eat at local restaurants, they keep a low profile. Unlike many politicians, Merkel is generally uninterested in talking with her constituents when she is not actively on duty.

Compared to her husband, however, Merkel is outgoing and enthusiastic. Ulrich Sauer guards his privacy very closely. While Merkel was campaigning in 2005, for example, Sauer refused to give any interviews that focused in any way on politics or his wife, though he would gladly speak about his scientific research. He also forbade his students from speaking with the media. He does not typically accompany Merkel on trips abroad and does not like to be photographed in political or government contexts; in one meeting of spouses of world leaders he attempted to avoid the cameras by hiding behind Laura Bush, the wife of former US president George W. Bush. Sauer even chose not to attend his wife's inauguration as chancellor in 2005, preferring to spend the day in his laboratory.

of Germany seem inclined to push her out of office. Her story remains a remarkable one. Despite growing up in the police state of East Germany, Merkel rose to become the leader of a democratic republic; despite growing up in an impoverished country, she came to be in charge of one of the world's wealthiest nations; and despite having shown little interest in politics and government in her youth, she moved quickly into leadership positions once elected. She has had a truly impressive career.

CHAPTER 5

Ellen Johnson Sirleaf

The 2005 presidential ballot in the West African country of Liberia contained a whopping twenty-two names. One of these candidates was Ellen Johnson Sirleaf, who was one of just two women on the ballot. Her chances of being elected seemed slim. No woman had ever been elected president in Liberia. Sirleaf, sixty-seven at the time, was one of the oldest candidates on the ballot, and she had made some influential political enemies. She had lived part of her life abroad, moreover, which put her beyond the currents of Liberian politics and made her vulnerable to charges of being an outsider. Finally, she had run for president eight years earlier and been soundly defeated.

The first-place finisher in this election was George Weah, a humanitarian and former soccer player who won 28 percent of the vote. Sirleaf, to the surprise of many observers, placed second, with 20 percent. The country's election rules, however, required a second round of voting because no candidate had received more than half the vote. Thus, the two top vote-getters, Weah and Sirleaf, faced each other in a runoff election. Weah's athletic feats and humanitarian works had made him a national hero. Most observers expected Sirleaf to fall short—again.

But when the ballots had been counted, Sirleaf's many talents, political experience, and tireless campaigning had carried the day. In the second round, she won almost 60 percent of the vote, easily defeating Weah. In January 2006 Sirleaf was inaugurated as Liberia's twenty-fourth president—and the first woman in any African country to be elected president or prime minister. She had made history.

From Africa to America

Ellen Johnson was born on October 29, 1938, in Liberia's capital city, Monrovia. Three of her grandparents were ethnically West African; the fourth was German. The German heritage made young Ellen lighter skinned than most of her peers. In a country where most people have dark skin, she stood out—and not in a good way. "Some of my classmates teased me about my complexion," she recalled years later in an autobiographical account. "They said I was too light to be a real African and called me Red Pumpkin, a name that hurt me to the bottom of my soul."[38] Many times, she wrote, she cried herself to sleep at night.

The Johnsons were reasonably well off. After elementary school, Ellen went on to high school at the most prestigious school in the country. She enjoyed sports, especially volleyball and table tennis, and did well academically. While a high school student, Johnson fell in love with James Sirleaf, a man several years older than her. Sirleaf was "tall and articulate, ambitious and charming and determined to succeed," she wrote in her autobiography, with "the scent of sophistication and adventure."[39] She overlooked signs that he might also be possessive. The couple married soon after she finished high school. Her family disapproved of the marriage; most girls of Ellen's background were traveling to the United States or elsewhere to attend college, and

> "Some of my classmates teased me about my complexion. They said I was too light to be a real African."[38]
>
> —Ellen Johnson Sirleaf

49

Ellen's parents wanted that for their daughter as well. But love won out.

The first years of the Sirleafs' marriage were difficult. Before long the couple had four sons. To save money, they moved in with James's mother. Ellen got a secretarial job, then moved on to a job as an assistant to an accountant. She discovered that she enjoyed finance, but she also felt that her life was going nowhere. Her friends were returning from college and moving on to exciting careers, while she seemed to have no particular future beyond motherhood and a succession of unfulfilling jobs. She was eager to study economics, but she lacked the money to make that possible.

When their youngest child was about a year old, James Sirleaf got a government scholarship to study in Wisconsin. Ellen seized the opportunity to apply for a scholarship herself, and through dogged persistence managed to obtain one. She enrolled in business courses in a college near where her husband would study. The couple left their children in the care of grandparents and flew to the United States in 1962. After earning a degree in accounting in Wisconsin, Ellen studied economics in Colorado and then enrolled at Harvard University in Massachusetts. The process took ten years, but at the end she had not only a bachelor's degree but a master's degree in public administration as well.

Minister of Finance

In 1971 the Sirleafs returned to Liberia. Their marriage, however, was nearly at an end. James Sirleaf had always been jealous where his wife was concerned, monitoring her activities closely; now he began behaving abusively toward Ellen. He slapped her once for working later than he wanted her to and once hit her with the handle of a gun. He was also often drunk. Ellen finally got the courage to leave him when he pointed a gun at her while one of their children looked on. "The boy grabbed a can of mosquito repellent and tried to spray it in his father's eyes,"[40] a reporter wrote.

After the marriage ended, Sirleaf moved on with her life. (James Sirleaf died in 1990.) Her educational experiences made her a good fit for government work. The president of Liberia in the

Inaugurated president of Liberia in 2006, Ellen Johnson Sirleaf was the first woman in history to be elected as prime minister or president of an African country. In a runoff election, she captured 60 percent of the vote against her opponent, former soccer great and humanitarian George Weah.

1970s was a man named William Tolbert, who had just taken office after the death of the previous president. Tolbert was searching for people to advise him, and he was impressed by Sirleaf's intelligence and background. He invited her to fill the position of Assistant Minister of Finance. Sirleaf was happy to take the position, which made good use of her economics background and her accounting skills. In particular, she was interested in finding ways to help the Liberian economy grow.

That was a thorny task. Corruption and bribery were widespread among government officials at all levels in Liberia. Despite holding an important government position, Sirleaf was powerless to change the country's culture of corruption. Instead she focused on Liberia's business community. She railed against Liberian corporations that invested their profits outside the country, for example, but had little success in convincing them to spend more money in Liberia. She argued with Tolbert at one point about government spending and resigned when she felt she was not being heard. In 1979 she returned, though, this time as Minister of Finance—a position that made her a full member of Tolbert's cabinet.

Violence and Arrest

That appointment almost cost Sirleaf her life. In 1980 an army officer named Samuel Doe led a military coup against Tolbert's regime. First, Doe and his followers broke into the president's house and killed Tolbert along with some of his supporters. Ten days later most members of Tolbert's cabinet were rounded up, tied to posts on a beach, and shot. "A crowd of thousands cheered," a reporter wrote, noting the unpopularity of the Tolbert regime, "and by all accounts there was jubilation throughout the country."[41]

Only four members of Tolbert's cabinet were spared. One of them was Sirleaf, who was placed under house arrest for a time. Exactly why she was not gunned down with most of the others remains unclear. One possibility is that Doe knew he would need her deep understanding of the country's finances going forward; another is that her family had at some point in the past done his family a kindness. Sirleaf's own comments over the years indicate that she does not know the reason.

Declaring himself president, Doe offered Sirleaf a job as head of a bank. She accepted the position but soon became critical of the degree of corruption in Doe's administration. She also disagreed with some of Doe's economic policies, which she believed were driving businesses out of Liberia. After speaking out publicly against him, she fled the country, fearing that Doe would seek re-

Liberia and Americo-Liberians

For many generations, the dominant group in Liberian politics consisted of so-called Americo-Liberians—the descendants of US slaves who had come to Liberia in the early 1800s to set up a new nation. Though no more than 5 percent of the Liberian population had American roots, nearly all presidents of the country have been Americo-Liberians—and most of the country's wealth has been in the hands of the Americo-Liberian elite as well.

Ellen Sirleaf is not Americo-Liberian. When she was young, this was a point against her. Even though the Johnsons had money and political connections, their ethnicity meant that they were not—and could never be—members of Liberia's inner circle. Simply serving in the cabinet of Americo-Liberian president William Tolbert, then, was an impressive achievement for a nonelite like Sirleaf. While the Americo-Liberian hold on the country lasted, Sirleaf's chances at reaching the presidency would have been slim at best.

Samuel Doe's coup put government in the hands of those who had never been part of the elite. In the wake of the coup, moreover, ordinary Liberians angrily blamed the Americo-Liberians for many of the woes of the country, driving some from Liberia altogether and forcing others to adopt a lower profile. For the first time in Liberian history, being an Americo-Liberian was a disadvantage. Indeed, while campaigning Sirleaf had to assure voters that she was not a member of the distrusted elite, as her educational levels and her well-off childhood might have suggested.

venge if she stayed. Eventually she settled in Kenya in East Africa. There she worked for an American bank for several years.

Sirleaf returned to Liberia in 1985. Doe had called for an election, and Sirleaf was asked by some Liberians to return home and run for vice president on an opposition ticket. Not long after she arrived she gave a speech critical of Doe and his advisers, whereupon Doe placed her under arrest. Though she was sentenced to a ten-year prison term, diplomats from other nations pressured Doe to pardon her, which he did before she had served any jail time. Doe won the election, helped by what most observers called massive election fraud. A month later, Sirleaf was arrested once more, following an attempted coup against Doe, though she was apparently not involved in the planning or carrying out of the revolt. This time she spent several months in prison before being released and fleeing the country.

Civil War

After working for several more years in banking, Sirleaf took a job with the United Nations in 1992. Her main responsibility was to help developing countries grow economically, and she served on several important committees as well. But her heart was in Liberia, which by this time was engaged in a ferocious civil war. When hostilities eased in 1997, she returned to the country and ran for president. Once again the election was controversial—once again, Sirleaf lost. She received just a quarter of the votes and left the country shortly afterward to return to her work with the UN.

A second civil war broke out two years after the election. The fighting left many Liberians dead and thousands more homeless. When the warring parties signed a peace treaty in 2003, Sirleaf returned to Liberia. The next presidential election was scheduled for 2005, and Sirleaf made it known that she would be a candidate. This time, she won. George Weah, her main opponent, asserted that Sirleaf had committed election fraud, but most observers said they had seen minor irregularities at most and called the election perfectly fair. One of Sirleaf's campaign aides argued that Weah knew full well that no fraud had been committed; the issue, she said, was that Weah's supporters "don't want a woman to be president in Africa."[42] Weah eventually withdrew his complaints, and in January 2006 Sirleaf took office.

> "Women are more committed. Women work harder. And women are more honest."[43]
>
> —Ellen Johnson Sirleaf

She had a difficult job ahead of her. The corruption endemic to Liberian society was still present and remained a huge drain on the country's economy and the people's trust in their government. About 80 percent of the population lived in abject poverty and only about 15 percent had jobs. Few Western corporations had much interest in opening branches or factories in Liberia,

Family Ties

To Ellen Johnson Sirleaf, one of the great features of Liberia is the close connection among family members—a connection that she benefited from enormously when she and her husband left Africa for Wisconsin. As she wrote in her memoir,

> In Liberia, as in all of Africa, parents routinely help their children care for the grandchildren—not just temporarily, not for a few hours or for the night but for weeks and months and even years. How routine is it for a Liberian woman to take her children to her parents and ask them to care for them because she has to work or go to school. No payment is given, no money left unless you happen to have it, which you probably do not. Whatever means the parents possess, however meager, are stretched to feed, shelter, and educate the grandchildren while the adult child goes off to improve herself.

> We left our boys with our families. . . . It was a heart-wrenching decision and a painful good-bye, especially with my youngest son. The separation created a hairline fracture in our relationship, the slightest of strains, that remains to this day. There was a time long ago, while we were talking and reminiscing about his childhood, that my youngest son paused me in a point and said, "But, Mom, you can't remember. You weren't there." Today, although we have become quite close, some guilt remains.

Ellen Johnson Sirleaf, *This Child Will Be Great.* New York: HarperCollins, 2009, p. 34.

and the country was deeply in debt to other nations. The violence of two civil wars, moreover, had razed villages and towns, killed thousands of Liberians, and forced one-third of the people to move into refugee camps.

Despite the overwhelming complications, Sirleaf believed that she was the right person for the job. She was prepared to battle the corruption in government; she had valuable experience in finance; and, in her opinion, women were simply better leaders than men. "Women are more committed," she said once. "Women work harder. And women are more honest."[43] She believed her age, too, would help. She was a grandmother by this time and expected that many Liberians would see her as a nurturing, kind leader.

Women

Sirleaf made improving the status of Liberia's women a major goal of her administration. She worked tirelessly for women's rights. Liberia had traditionally been a very dangerous place for women. Rape was common, and penalties for it almost nonexistent. Domestic violence was widespread. Women made up a disproportionate number of the poor and unemployed. In response, Sirleaf set up new justice courts to encourage women who had been raped to come forward, and she established programs to train women for jobs.

Her work in this area did not go unnoticed. In 2011 Sirleaf and two other women were awarded the coveted Nobel Peace Prize. All three honorees earned their award specifically for their work with women. As the Nobel committee wrote, the prize was given to the recipients "for their non-violent struggle for the safety of women and for women's rights to full participation in peace-building work."[44] The award brought Sirleaf attention not only in Liberia but around the world as well.

In other areas, Sirleaf's efforts at reform proved more difficult. "I beg you I no magician," she explained once, using common Liberian speech. "I can't just wave a magic wand."[45] The corruption culture persisted despite her attempts to eliminate it. If she were to fire all the openly corrupt officials, she once noted, not enough people would remain to do the work. Economically, too, things did not improve as quickly as Sirleaf had hoped. By the end of her term in 2011, little progress had been made in combating poverty and bringing in jobs.

> "I beg you I no magician. I can't just wave a magic wand."[45]
>
> —Ellen Johnson Sirleaf

Sirleaf had originally promised to serve just one presidential term. As the end of her tenure approached, however, she changed her mind. A single six-year term, she decided, was

Along with two others, Sirleaf was awarded the Nobel Peace Prize in 2011 in recognition of her efforts to improve the status of women. Her work in this realm included establishing job-training programs and setting up new justice courts to aid female sexual assault victims.

not enough time to bring about the changes she had hoped for. As a result she decided to run again in 2011. The election was close. She won 44 percent of the vote in the first round and was forced into a runoff, which she won handily when her main opponent, charging that Sirleaf's camp had committed voter fraud, boycotted the second round altogether. She moved into her second six-year term intent, as before, on improving her country in whatever way she could. The odds may still be against Ellen Sirleaf, but then again she has overcome the odds on many occasions before. Time will tell how she fares with this difficult task.

CHAPTER 6

Hillary Clinton

The wife of the US president is called the First Lady. Most First Ladies have been overshadowed by their husbands, but a few, such as Eleanor Roosevelt, the wife of Franklin Roosevelt, had achievements that brought them attention in their own right. But no First Lady has been as prominent as Hillary Clinton. Between 1993 and 2001, when her husband, Bill Clinton, was in office, Hillary Clinton was active in making and setting policy in a way unequaled by any previous First Lady. After Bill left office, Hillary ran for the US Senate and won. In 2009 she left the Senate to take on the role of Secretary of State. And as of early 2016, she was a leading contender for the presidency. Her career has been extraordinary by any standard.

Republicans and Democrats

Hillary Clinton was born Hillary Rodham in Chicago on October 26, 1947. She grew up mainly in suburban Park Ridge. Her father owned a business, and her mother was a homemaker. An excellent student, Hillary was involved in many activities throughout her elementary and high school years. She won a number of awards as a Girl Scout and played on sports teams in addition to being a reporter for her high school newspaper and a member of the student council. When she finished high school in 1965, her classmates voted her the member of the class who was most likely to be successful.

Hillary was also active in politics during her teenage years. Her upbringing was solidly Republican. At age thirteen she was involved in the 1960 presidential election—she supported the Republican candidate, Richard Nixon—and campaigned four years later for another Republican, Barry Goldwater. At the same time, Hillary had liberal influences in her life as well, particularly at her church. In 1962, for example, she and her youth minister had the good fortune to meet Martin Luther King Jr.

Following high school, Hillary enrolled at Wellesley College in Massachusetts. She chose to major in political science and became president of the Young Republicans, a student organization devoted to electing Republican candidates. The beginning of her college career coincided with two important political movements. One was the start of protests against American involvement in the Vietnam War, which was being fought against Communist North Vietnam in Asia. The other was the growth of the Civil Rights Movement, in which African Americans lobbied for equal treatment with whites.

Hillary was drawn to both of these movements. She saw each as an example of social justice in action: both the antiwar protesters and the civil rights activists, in her opinion, were doing what was morally and ethically right. She also noticed that both movements were led primarily by liberals and Democrats. Though Hillary continued to work in the campaigns of more liberal Republicans for several years, she drifted gradually toward the Democratic Party. By the election of November 1968, she was squarely in the Democratic camp.

College and Law School

At Wellesley, Hillary was known as a leader. She was elected president of student government in 1968, and she organized a student strike that year in the wake of Martin Luther King's assassination; she and other students pushed for changes in the college's admissions and hiring practices for the benefit of African Americans. It was not traditional for students to speak at Wellesley graduations, but Hillary's classmates convinced college officials to allow a student speaker. Unsurprisingly, Hillary Rodham was chosen to represent the class. As the college president noted, "There was no debate so far as I could ascertain as to who their spokesman was to be."[46]

> "There was no debate so far as I could ascertain as to who their spokesman was to be."[46]
>
> —Wellesley College president on Hillary Rodham.

Hillary then enrolled at Yale Law School and took particular interest in issues involving children. After getting her law degree, she studied for another year at the Yale Child Study Center; her research culminated in the publication of a scholarly article, "Children Under the Law." Following her time at Yale, she moved to Washington, DC, where she was active in the movement to impeach—or remove from office—president Richard Nixon. Just as at Wellesley, many people recognized Hillary's intelligence and persistence, and at least one political consultant thought she could easily become a senator, perhaps even president.

Hillary Rodham might have stayed in Washington for good, but she chose a different path. While at law school she had met Bill Clinton, a fellow student whose interest in government and politics was as great as her own. They began dating in 1971 and were soon a couple. At first, Hillary refused Bill's offers of marriage. Bill planned to return to his native Arkansas to launch a political career; Hillary knew that marrying Bill would mean leaving Washington, a city where her career prospects were superior. But in 1974, Hillary moved to Arkansas and got a job teaching at a law school. The following year, Bill and Hillary were married.

First Lady

In 1976, the year Bill Clinton was elected state attorney general, Hillary began working for a law firm, where she specialized in legal issues involving children and families. One commentator has called her "one of the most important scholar-activists"[47] of the time. In 1977 she cofounded a group that advocated for the well-being of Arkansas's children. A year later, Bill was elected governor of the state; two years after that, the Clintons' only child, Chelsea, was born. Hillary continued to work for her law firm during her husband's governorship. She also served on corporate boards and kept advocating on behalf of children and families.

With Hillary's support, Bill Clinton ran for the presidency in 1992. It was clear that Hillary would play an important role in her husband's presidency if he were to be elected. Indeed, Bill Clinton told voters that they would get "two for the price of one"[48] by casting their ballots in his favor. Some voters were fine with that, pointing out that Hillary had a strong background in law and government. Others disagreed, arguing that Hillary was unelected and should not be involved in her husband's administration.

Hillary Clinton campaigns alongside her husband, future president Bill Clinton, in 1992. As Bill was finishing his second term in office, Hillary moved from the couple's home state of Arkansas to New York and successfully ran for the US Senate in 2000.

Hillary Clinton also made a number of controversial comments during the campaign, bringing her unwanted attention. In a televised interview, for example, she seemed to disparage women who chose to raise children full-time instead of joining the workforce. "I suppose I could have stayed home and baked cookies and had teas," she told the interviewer, "but what I decided to do was to fulfill my profession which I entered before my husband was in public life."[49] She explained later that she had not meant to criticize anyone else's decisions, adding that the goal of feminism was to permit women a broad range of choices. Nonetheless, comments like these alienated many tradition-minded voters.

A Political Childhood

In 1960 Chicago mayor Richard J. Daley was accused by Republicans (including Hillary Rodham's father) of stealing the presidential election for his candidate, John F. Kennedy. In her memoir Clinton described how she and a friend—eighth graders at the time—worked with a group looking for evidence that Daley had committed fraud.

The ad called for volunteers to gather at a downtown hotel at 9 A.M. on a Saturday morning. Betsy and I . . . knew our parents would never give us permission, so we didn't ask. We took the bus downtown, walked to the hotel and were directed into a small ballroom. . . We were each handed a stack of voter registration lists and assigned to different teams who, we were told, would drive us to our destinations, drop us off and pick us up a few hours later.

Betsy and I separated and went off with total strangers. I ended up with a couple who drove me to the South Side, dropped me off in a poor neighborhood and told me to knock on doors and ask people their names so I could compare them with registration lists. . . . Off I went, fearless and stupid. I did find a vacant lot that was listed as the address for about a dozen alleged voters. . . . When I finished, I stood on the corner waiting to be picked up, happy that I'd ferreted out proof of my father's contention that "Daley stole the election for Kennedy."

—Hillary Clinton, *Living History.* New York: Simon and Schuster, 2003, p. 17.

Bill Clinton won election easily in 1992, and Hillary Clinton became First Lady. She was immediately chosen to lead a committee that would overhaul the way Americans bought health insurance. The committee came up with a plan that would extend health coverage to many more Americans and at the same time would involve the government more than ever before. Some Americans loved the plan; others despised it. In the end, the plan did not become law. The First Lady did have success in implementing other policies, however, such as reforming adoption laws, calling attention to domestic violence, and improving conditions for children in foster care.

Bill Clinton served two terms as president. Each term had its share of controversy. During the first term both Clintons were under investigation for their business dealings in Arkansas. Hillary Clinton was also criticized for firing a number of White House employees and replacing them with her friends. Both of these controversies were widely reported, and each damaged the First Lady's popularity. But in 1998, when Bill Clinton admitted to having had an affair with a White House intern, Hillary Clinton's popularity soared. Many viewed her sympathetically as an innocent victim of her husband's indiscretion. She considered leaving the marriage, but ultimately did not. "No one understands me better and no one can make me laugh the way Bill does,"[50] she wrote in her memoir.

Senator Clinton

Even before Bill Clinton's presidency came to an end, Hillary was running for the US Senate from New York. The Clintons bought a house north of New York City, and Hillary set out to convince voters that she could represent them despite never having lived in the state. Toward this end, she visited all of New York's counties; held open meetings with voters; and talked to reporters, mayors, and civic leaders about the issues. Her hard work paid off: she won the election easily. Clinton generally voted with other Democrats, voting against the Republican Party's tax plans, for example. But Clinton did not always take the liberal position. Most notably, in the wake of the 9/11 terrorist attacks she voted to authorize President George W. Bush to attack Iraq if he believed war was necessary— a decision that earned her criticism from antiwar activists.

Clinton coasted to reelection in 2006, but she already had bigger plans in mind: the presidency. She knew that few Democrats could match her experience in politics and government. Moreover, most Democratic voters held a positive view of her. And Clinton was widely considered a strong voice in favor of equality, fairness, and the rights of women and minorities. Her fundamental message to Americans, she said at one point, was a simple one: "Let's stay true to our values. Let's continue to stand up for those who are vulnerable to being left out or marginalized."[51] As she saw it, this message would resound with a large percentage of the electorate. Accordingly, Clinton announced her intention to run for the Democratic nomination in 2008. Her primary challenger was Illinois senator Barack Obama, whose message of hope and change seemed to resonate with Democratic voters more than Clinton's. In the end the nominee was Obama.

> "Let's continue to stand up for those who are vulnerable to being left out or marginalized."[51]
>
> —Hillary Clinton

Despite the loss, Clinton had come much closer than any woman to winning the presidential nomination of a major American political party. Clinton accepted her defeat and campaigned hard for Obama in the fall. When Obama won the presidency, he asked Clinton to join his cabinet as Secretary of State. Clinton was doubtful at first. The campaign had been grueling, she was not sure she wanted to try something new, and she was enjoying her work in the Senate. Ultimately, she decided to accept the challenge, which she called a "difficult and exciting adventure."[52] Though Clinton was not the first woman to serve as Secretary of State, she was the first former First Lady to hold a cabinet post.

A Cabinet Position

As Secretary of State, Clinton concentrated on building strong connections with other nations. In particular, she tried to develop stronger ties with Russia and Pakistan, two nations whose relations with the United States had often been shaky. At the same time, Clinton showed a willingness to use diplomacy to punish and isolate countries, such as Iran, that she considered potential threats. A strong believer in talking with people in person, she visited over a hundred countries in her time as Secretary of State. "She checks on the issues she cares about, deeply and specifically,"[53] reported one of her assistants.

Not everything went well during Clinton's tenure in the State Department. In 2012 a US diplomatic base in Benghazi, Libya, was attacked. Four Americans died, including the US ambassador to Libya. Asked to investigate what happened, a panel of experts concluded that the State Department had not provided enough security in an unstable and unfriendly country. Clinton

Clinton testifies at a congressional committee hearing about events that took place during her tenure as Secretary of State: a US diplomatic base in Benghazi, Libya, was attacked, and four Americans were killed. Although Clinton took responsibility for errors in judgment that led to the attacks, many of her political foes remained convinced she was lying about her actions.

A Polarizing Influence

More than almost any other political leader, Hillary Clinton has had a polarizing influence on the American public. Since being elected to the Senate, Clinton has been looked at favorably by about half of all voters—and unfavorably by most of the rest. Very few people view her neutrally; polls consistently show that no more than 5 percent of Americans hold no opinion of Clinton. Indeed, in a book titled *Hillary Rodham Clinton: Polarizing First Lady*, historian Gil Troy argues that Clinton "has been uniquely controversial and contradictory since she first appeared on the national radar screen" and that she has "alternately fascinated, bedeviled, bewitched, and appalled Americans."

The split in perception largely reflects the division between liberals and conservatives. Many Republicans see Clinton as a symbol of all of the nation's ills; right-wing fund-raising appeals often warn potential donors that failure to give generously could lead to a Clinton presidency. Many Democrats, in contrast, are staunch supporters of Clinton and her policies. However, support and opposition do sometimes cross party lines: Some Republican women are admirers of Clinton, while many on the far left wing of the Democratic Party believe that she is too conservative on economic issues.

Gil Troy, *Hillary Rodham Clinton: Polarizing First Lady.* Lawrence, KS: University Press of Kansas, 2006, p. 4.

took responsibility for the deaths and the errors in judgment that led to them. Many Republicans in Congress, however, thought Clinton was lying about her actions and opened further inquiry; as of early 2016, investigations continued.

Clinton also ran into trouble for using a private e-mail server to conduct some State Department business. Some of her opponents have charged that this decision may have resulted in the leaking of classified information, though no one has yet demonstrated that this was the case. Others have wondered whether Clinton was trying to conceal shady activities by keeping certain e-mails from being made public. Clinton has consistently denied any wrongdoing. She has argued that she handled e-mail in the same way as other Secretaries of State, including Colin Powell, who had served under Republican president George W. Bush. She also flatly denied that any classified information was included in the e-mails in question. Again, investigations continue.

An Eye on the Presidency

When Obama won a second term as president in 2012, Clinton stepped down as Secretary of State. For the time being, at least, she was tired of what she called "the high wire of American politics"[54] and wanted some time away from government after years of being constantly in the public eye. She was also mulling over a possible presidential run in 2016. She was one of the best-known politicians on the planet, she was rated favorably by most Democratic voters, and her tenure as Secretary of State had given her valuable experience in foreign affairs.

In April 2015, following months of speculation that she would run, Clinton officially announced her candidacy for the Democratic nomination. "Everyday Americans need a champion," she said in her announcement speech, "So I'm hitting the road to earn your vote—because it's your time. And I hope you'll join me on this journey."[55] She immediately started meeting with voters in Iowa, the first state to make a selection in the 2016 primary season, and soon traveled to other states as well to talk to politicians, community and business leaders, and ordinary citizens. As of early 2016 Clinton had the endorsement of the vast majority of Democrats in Congress and was locked in a tight race for her party's nomination.

> "She checks on the issues she cares about, deeply and specifically."[53]
>
> —Assistant to Secretary of State Hillary Clinton.

Whatever happens in Clinton's race for the presidency, her place in history is assured. Simply serving as Secretary of State is an impressive achievement; coupling that with winning two elections for the Senate makes Clinton's accomplishments even more remarkable. And her ability to mount a serious campaign for president puts her in a category by herself. No American woman can equal Clinton's record of service to her country.

SOURCE NOTES

Introduction: Queens and Beyond

1. Quoted in *BBC Radio,* "Elizabethan Echoes," March 24, 2003. www.bbc.co.uk.
2. Quoted in Torild Skard, *Women of Power*. London: Policy Press, 2015, p. 10.

Chapter 1: Indira Gandhi

3. Quoted in Helen Pidd, "Why Is India So Bad for Women?," *Guardian* (Manchester), July 23, 2012. www.theguardian.com.
4. Quoted in Pranay Gupte, *Mother India: A Political Biography of Indira Gandhi*. New Delhi, India: Penguin Books India, 2009, p. 143.
5. Quoted in Dom Moraes, *Mrs. Gandhi*. London: J. Cape, 1980, p. 72.
6. Quoted in Linda Charlton, "Assassination in India," *New York Times*, November 1, 1984. www.nytimes.com.
7. Moraes, *Mrs. Gandhi*, p. 102.
8. "India: The Lady vs. the Syndicate," *Time*, August 29, 1969. http://content.time.com.
9. Quoted in BBC, "On This Day," June 12, 2008. http://news.bbc.co.uk.
10. Quoted in Charlton, "Assassination in India."
11. Quoted in Charlton, "Assassination in India."
12. Quoted in Kailash Dubey, "Last Speech of Indira Gandhi," *Times of Congress* (New Delhi), April 6, 2014. www.timesofcongress.com.

Chapter 2: Golda Meir

13. Quoted in Hela Crown-Tamir, *Israel, History in a Nutshell.* Jerusalem, Israel: TsurTsina, 2012, p. 137.
14. Quoted in Israel Shenker, "Golda Meir: Peace and Arab Acceptance Were Goals of Her 5 Years as Premier," *New York Times,* December 9, 1978. www.nytimes.com.
15. Quoted in Steven Joel Rubin, *Writing Our Lives: Autobiographies of American Jews, 1890–1990.* Philadelphia: Jewish Publication Society, 1991, p. 94.
16. Quoted in Skard, *Women of Power*, p. 32.
17. Quoted in Richard Amdur, *Golda Meir: A Leader in Peace and War.* New York: Fawcett Columbine, 1990, p. 61.
18. Quoted in Shenker, "Golda Meir: Peace and Arab Acceptance Were Goals of Her 5 Years as Premier."
19. Quoted in Asaf Siniver, ed., *The Yom Kippur War.* New York: Oxford University Press, 2013, p. 39.
20. Quoted in Abraham Rabinovich, "Three Years Too Late, Golda Meir Understood How War Could Have Been Avoided," *Times of Israel*, September 12, 2013. www.timesofisrael.com.
21. Quoted in Shenker, "Golda Meir: Peace and Arab Acceptance Were Goals of Her 5 Years as Premier."

Chapter 3: Margaret Thatcher

22. Quoted in *Guardian* (Manchester), "Margaret Thatcher: A Life in Quotes," April 8, 2013. www.theguardian.com.
23. Quoted in Joseph R. Gregory, "Margaret Thatcher, 'Iron Lady' Who Set Britain on New Course, Dies at 87," *New York Times,* April 8, 2013. www.nytimes.com.
24. Quoted in David Runciman, "Rat-a-tat-a-tat-a-tat-a-tat," *London Review of Books,* June 6, 2013. www.lrb.co.uk.
25. Quoted in Lizette Alvarez, "Sir Denis Thatcher, 88, Dies," *New York Times*, June 27, 2003. www.nytimes.com.
26. Quoted in Ann Hui, "Thatcherisms," *Globe and Mail* (Toronto), April 8, 2013. www.theglobeandmail.com.
27. Quoted in Rebecca Smith, "How Margaret Thatcher Became Known as 'Milk Snatcher,'" *Telegraph* (London), August 8, 2010. www.telegraph.co.uk.
28. Margaret Thatcher, "Britain Awake," Margaret Thatcher Foundation, January 19, 1976. www.margaretthatcher.org.

29. Quoted in Chris Abbott, *21 Speeches That Shaped Our World*. New York: Random House, 2010, p. 196.

Chapter 4: Angela Merkel

30. Quoted in Skard, *Women of Power*, p. 422.
31. Quoted in Franziska Augstein, "How Angela Merkel Became Europe's Undisputed Leader," *Guardian* (Manchester), February 15, 2015. www.theguardian.com.
32. Quoted in George Packer, "The Quiet German," *New Yorker*, December 1, 2014. www.newyorker.com.
33. Quoted in Packer, "The Quiet German."
34. Justin Huggler, "10 Moments That Define German Chancellor Angela Merkel," *Telegraph* (London), October 9, 2015. www.telegraph.co.uk.
35. Quoted in Packer, "The Quiet German."
36. Sara Miller Llana, "The Mind of Angela Merkel," *Christian Science Monitor*, September 20, 2013. www.csmonitor.com.
37. Quoted in Will Hutton, "Angela Merkel's Humane Stance on Immigration Is a Lesson to Us All," *Guardian* (Manchester), August 30, 2015. www.theguardian.com.

Chapter 5: Ellen Johnson Sirleaf

38. Ellen Johnson Sirleaf, *This Child Will Be Great.* New York: HarperCollins, 2009, p. 27.
39. Sirleaf, *This Child Will Be Great*, p. 45.
40. Daniel Bergner, "An Uncompromising Woman," *New York Times Magazine*, October 22, 2010. www.nytimes.com.
41. Sanford J. Ungar, "Liberia," *Atlantic*, June 1981. www.theatlantic.com.
42. Quoted in Todd Pitman, "Liberian May Be Africa's 1st Elected Woman President," Boston.com, November 11, 2005. www.boston.com.
43. Quoted in Bergner, "An Uncompromising Woman."
44. Nobelprize.org, "The Nobel Peace Prize 2011." www.nobelprize.org.
45. Quoted in Bergner, "An Uncompromising Woman."

Chapter 6: Hillary Clinton

46. Wellesley College, "Hillary D. Rodham's 1969 Student Commencement Speech." www.wellesley.edu.

47. Quoted in Sue Thomas and Clyde Wilcox, eds., *Women and Elective Office: Past, Present, and Future*. New York: Oxford University Press, 2014, p. 82.

48. Quoted in Peter W. Schramm, ed., *Consequences of the Clinton Victory*. Ashland, OH: Ashbrook Press, 1994, p. 81.

49. Quoted in *Nightline Transcripts*, "Making Hillary Clinton an Issue," March 26, 1992. www.pbs.org.

50. Hillary Rodham Clinton, *Living History*. New York: Simon & Schuster, 2003, p. 75.

51. Quoted in Gayle Tzemach Lemmon, "Hillary Clinton's War for Women's Rights." The Daily Beast, March 6, 2011. www.thedailybeast .com.

52. Quoted in Scott J. Anderson, Ed Henry, and Kristi Keck, "Clinton Wants to Be Part of Obama's 'Exciting Adventure,'" CNN.com, December 1, 2008.

53. Quoted in Lemmon, "Hillary Clinton's War for Women's Rights."

54. Quoted in Karen DeYoung, "Clinton: Done with the 'High Wire' of Politics. Really.," *Washington Post*, January 26, 2012. www.wash ingtonpost.com.

55. Quoted in Amy Chozick, "Hillary Clinton Announces 2016 Presidential Bid," *New York Times*, April 12, 2015. www.nytimes.com.

FOR FURTHER RESEARCH

Books

David A. Adler, *Golda Meir: A Strong, Determined Leader.* New York: Puffin, 2015.

Craig E. Blohm, *Hillary Clinton*. San Diego, CA: ReferencePoint, 2016.

Tonya Cupp, *Angela Merkel.* London: Cavendish Square, 2014.

Michelle Roehm McCann and Amelie Welden, *Girls Who Rocked the World: Heroines from Joan of Arc to Mother Teresa.* New York: Aladdin, 2012.

Claire Throp, *Angela Merkel.* London: Raintree, 2014.

Internet Resources

Margaret Thatcher Foundation, "Margaret Thatcher Foundation." www .margaretthatcher.org.

Nobelprize.org, "The Nobel Peace Prize 2011." www.nobelprize.org /nobel_prizes/peace/laureates/2011/.

George Packer, "The Quiet German," *New Yorker*, December 1, 2014. www.newyorker.com/magazine/2014/12/01/quiet-german.

Letty Cottin Pogrebin, "Golda Meir," Jewish Women's Archive. http://jwa.org/encyclopedia/article/meir-golda.

The White House, "Hillary Rodham Clinton." www.whitehouse.gov/1600/first-ladies/hillaryclinton.

INDEX

PICTURE CREDITS

ABOUT THE AUTHOR

Stephen Currie has written dozens of books for children and young adults, including *Evolution* and *Cyberbullying* for Reference-Point Press. He has also taught at grade levels from kindergarten to college. He lives in the Hudson Valley of New York State.